Kentucky Spirited Treasures

Kentucky Spirited Treasures
BOURBON, WINE & 'SHINE

by The Kentucky Spirited Chef | Dayna Seelig

ISBN 978-0-578-52530-3

Cover design and book layout by
Jeffrey Liles, Mound Marketing & Communications LLC

Photography by
Dayna Seelig
Dylan Lambert, Dylan Lambert Photography

Published in association with
IngramSpark

Note to reader: Cup measurements in this book are for U.S. cups. Teaspoons are 5 ml and tablespoons are 15 ml. Temperatures are in Fahrenheit degrees. Conversion charts can be found in the index. All cooking times are an approximate guide only. Unless otherwise stated, milk is assumed to be whole, eggs are large and pepper is freshly ground black pepper.

Disclaimer: This book assumes the reader does not suffer from any food allergies or related medical conditions. Anyone with a food allergy should avoid recipes that contain ingredients which could cause an adverse reaction in the reader or anyone who will eat the prepared food.

This publication is intended only for responsible adults of legal drinking age in the U.S. (21 years old or older). It is intended solely for entertainment purposes. The author and publisher do not advocate or encourage the abuse of alcoholic beverages. Please drink responsibly and with moderation. Please do NOT drink and drive. We do not, under any circumstances, accept responsibility for any damages that result to yourself or anyone else due to the consumption of alcoholic beverages.

Although the author and publisher have made every effort to ensure that the information in this book was correct at press time, the author and publisher do not assume and hereby disclaim any liability to any party for any loss, damage, or disruption caused by errors or omissions, whether such errors or omissions result from negligence, accident, or any other cause.

Dedication

I dedicate this book to my amazing husband, Mike, who walks beside me each day, loving me and providing unwavering support for all of my new adventures! Thank you for editing, reading, listening, providing your honest opinion about each dish and for encouraging my creative cuisine. You are my best friend in the world and champion taste-tester. I love and appreciate you more than you will ever know!

—Dayna

Acknowledgements

Thank you to photographer, Dylan Lambert, for taking the most creative photos in some of the most beautiful gardens, homes and unusual settings! Your photos make me want to cry - in a good way!

A very special thank you to Frances Roberts for opening her gardens and historic home to photograph outdoor scenes for the book. And thank you to Elaine Crocket, Frances Roberts' daughter, for providing historical information about the Roberts house.

A very special thank you to Judge and Mrs. Todd Walton for allowing me to spend an evening photographing food on your beautiful porch. It has made a breathtakingly beautiful photo for the front of the book and it is always wonderful to visit with my talented cousins!

A very special thank you to Jane Anne Clark. I appreciate how graciously you said "do anything you want; move anything you want" in order to capture the breakfast scenes on your beautiful grounds and rock patio. I wish I could have my breakfast there every day! And I would bring you blueberry peach scones.

A loving thank you to my mother, Carol Spencer, for her artistic eye, creative table arrangements and beautiful flower designs in the book. And for always believing in me and encouraging me in my wild endeavors.

Thank you to Carol Hayes and Becky Priest for attending the impromptu garden party to taste test food. You both are always ready to cheer me on and be part of my cookbook experience.

It is with special appreciation that I thank Jeffrey Liles for editing, layout expertise and guidance throughout the whole publishing process. Without your generosity, your expertise and support this book would not exist. You have been the perfect collaboration partner!

Thank you to Carmen Liles for thoughtfully reading, reviewing and providing suggestions for clarity as well as accepting "Dayna's door-to-door dessert delivery service". Your eye for detail is amazing and the book is so much better for your suggestions.

Thank you to the taste testing party guests who thoughtfully tested 15 foods and a drink in 2 hours. I appreciate your stamina and honest feedback that helped me fine tune the final few recipes for the book.

And thank you to all of the individuals who pick up this book and are inspired to make one of the recipes. I hope you enjoy preparing and sharing them with friends and family who make your life richer as much as I have enjoyed creating them.

Contents

The pitcher shown here belonged to my Great-Great-Aunt Cora. My family uses this and many other heirloom dishes whenever we get together. I believe beautiful items should be a part of everyday meals, rather than tucked away for safekeeping. We always enjoy sharing stories about our relatives when people ask, "Where did you find that?"

Introduction

Kentucky has a rich history of producing spirits. Moonshine was a source of illicit income in the Appalachian region for many years during the 20th Century. In 2010 the government legalized moonshine products allowing for wide distribution.

The first commercial vineyard in the United States was planted along the Kentucky River and currently more than 60 wineries or vineyards are producing grapes and/or wine for sale.

And Kentucky is the birthplace for bourbon, which is America's only native spirit. To be called bourbon, it must be made with at least 51% corn and must be made in the United States with very exacting standards.

These spirited treasures began in Kentucky and they play an integral role in our heritage, agriculture, families and cuisine. During prohibition distillers provided "liquid refreshment" to those who knew how to make a connection, and speakeasys dotted the countryside.

Kentucky currently boasts wine and bourbon festivals; the Kentucky Bourbon Trail ™; vineyard tours; and Kentucky Proud products made with bourbon, wine and moonshine.

Kentucky has a rich and diverse culinary heritage drawing from many regions and cultures. Many of my family's historic recipes called for a "a teacup" or "lots of butter" as part of the list of ingredients, but now have been revised to include measurements we all recognize.

All recipes are carefully chosen and tested dishes that use Kentucky spirits. This book includes both new creations and old family recipes – guaranteed to become new favorites of your family and guests.

On The Cover

The photo on the cover of this book was taken at the home of Judge and Mrs. Todd Walton in Flemingsburg, Ky.

The home was built in 1910 and the Walton's have called it home since 1988.

The two wicker swings on the wraparound porch are always in use by their grandchildren and occasionally by my mother when she stops by to visit the Waltons – or even when no one is at home!

The house has a hidden gazebo retreat nestled next to a large magnolia tree, making it the perfect location to sip, eat and relax on a summer afternoon.

Appetizers
& Starters

Baked Brie with Peach Bourbon

1 sheet puff pastry, thawed

8 to 12 oz round brie

½ cup peach preserves or jam

2 Tbsp peach bourbon

2 Tbsp chopped walnuts

1 egg beaten

Unfold thawed puff pastry onto a lightly floured surface or parchment paper.

Slice the top rind off the brie and set the brie in the middle of the puff pastry.

Mix the jam and peach bourbon together until smooth and spoon on top of the brie.

Top with chopped walnuts.

Fold the puff pastry to cover the brie, using your hands to make sure it is firmly against the sides.

Brush the pastry lightly with a beaten egg. (Do not let the pastry sit in any egg that has run down the sides.)

Bake at 375 degrees on a baking sheet with parchment paper for about 35 minutes. Let it sit at room temperature for about 10 minutes before serving.

Transfer to a serving plate and garnish with crackers, fruit or crostini.

Adult Hot Chocolate

For each serving

5 oz whole milk

1 serving dark hot chocolate mix

3 oz bourbon cream

Serves 8

Bourbon Whipped Cream

1 cup heavy cream, chilled

1 ½ Tbsp bourbon

1 tsp sugar

For hot chocolate: Mix whole milk with the dark hot chocolate mix. Whisk well.

Place in microwave for 90 seconds or until steaming.

Remove from microwave and add bourbon cream. Whisk well again and heat for 30 seconds more in microwave.

For Bourbon Whipped Cream: Whip the heavy cream with a mixer until stiff peaks form.

Stir in bourbon and sugar and immediately top the hot chocolate in the cup with the Bourbon Whipped Cream.

Even as a child I passed on hot chocolate when it was offered. As much as I loved chocolate I never liked it with hot milk. However, I guarantee all "adult kids" will love this version made with milk and bourbon cream. Better than a hot toddy for an evening drink!

—Dayna

Bourbon Maple Bacon Bites

10 slices bacon

8 oz tube crescent dough sheet

¼ cup maple syrup

2 Tbsp bourbon

¾ cup brown sugar

Bake the bacon until crispy. Drain it well and press paper towels on the bacon while it is still warm to remove as much grease as possible. Crumble into small pieces.

Preheat oven to 375 degrees.

TIP: Line a large cookie sheet with non-stick foil. You will be so glad you did not skip this suggestion!

Roll out the crescent dough sheet on the lined cookie sheet. Do not stretch. Make sure there are no holes.

Mix maple syrup, bourbon, and just ½ cup of the brown sugar together.

Brush the crescent dough sheet with ½ of the mixture. Layer with the bacon pieces. Drizzle the remaining ½ of the mixture on top of the bacon, keeping the bacon spread out evenly.

Using the remaining ¼ cup of brown sugar, lightly sprinkle over the bacon.

Bake until the pastry is done and the mixture on top is bubbling. Approximately 15-20 minutes. Do not underbake the pastry. It should be crisp on the bottom when it cools.

Cut into bite-sized squares after the dish has cooled. While it will be hard to wait, the taste is best at room temperature.

Cheese and Andouille Appetizer Plate

Savory Cheese Appetizer Plate

8 oz Monterey Jack cheese, sliced

8 oz sharp cheddar cheese, sliced

4 green onion tops, sliced thin

2 oz crumbled feta cheese

¼ cup shredded three cheese blend

6 oz Spicy Chili Bacon Jam

2 Tbsp bourbon

Andouille Bites

¾ lb andouille sausage, sliced ½ inch thick on diagonal

1 ½ Tbsp olive oil, use garlic olive oil if you have it

2 Tbsp minced garlic

1 tsp bourbon smoked paprika

2 Tbsp red wine

1 tsp dried thyme

Serving suggestions: Serve with cheese or on a toothpick along with pineapple. It can also be an item on an antipasto plate.

Arrange sliced cheese on the plate, alternating colors.

Mix Spicy Chili Bourbon Jam with 2 Tbsp bourbon. The bourbon should thin the jam so it is easily drizzled across the cheese. It can also be put in a microwave for 10 seconds. Note: You do not want it like a liquid, only just thin enough to drizzle.

Sprinkle the three cheese blend, feta and sliced green onions on top for a quick and easy appetizer.

TIP: The Spicy Chili Bacon Jam makes the cheese special. If you cannot find Spicy Chili Bacon Jam already prepared, combine 2 oz of Thai chili wing sauce with 4 oz of bacon jam.

For the Andouille Bites: Heat olive oil in large skillet. Place andouille sausage in a single layer in the skillet. Lightly brown pieces on both sides. When the second side is browned, drain on a paper towel.

Add garlic, bourbon smoked paprika, wine and dried thyme to the skillet and mix well.

Add drained sausage back in the skillet and cook for one more minute to coat with the seasoning. Stir often to keep from sticking.

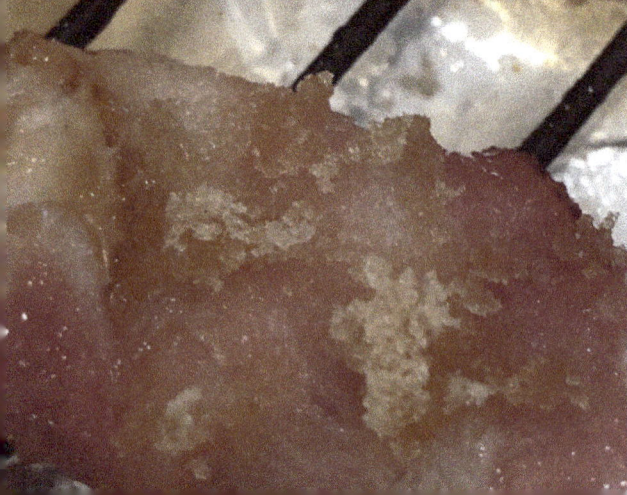

Everything is better with bacon. Add some bourbon and brown sugar and you have an appetizer that will disappear fast. And just between you and me, you don't have to tell your guests how easy they were to make!

Chicken Bacon Wraps

3 chicken breasts

9 pieces center cut bacon

Olive oil spray

Salt and pepper

½ cup maple syrup

¾ cup brown sugar

2 Tbsp bourbon

TIP: It is important to use a grate and foil on the pan or the bottom of the chicken will be soggy. Brush on the syrup, brown sugar and bourbon mixture on both sides first before topping with the remaining brown sugar.

A baking rack or roasting pan with a rack is needed for this recipe. Line the pan with aluminum foil for easy clean up.

Cut each chicken breast in three pieces lengthwise, then cut each piece in half.

Spray chicken pieces with olive oil spray, then salt and pepper lightly. Turn each piece over and repeat.

Cut each piece of bacon in half.

Wrap each piece of chicken with the half piece of bacon and place it on baking rack with the ends of the bacon on the bottom.

Bake at 375 degrees until the bacon is fully cooked around the chicken.

Mix maple syrup, ½ cup of the brown sugar, and 2 Tbsp bourbon together.

Using a brush, baste the chicken and bacon with the mixture about midway through at about 10 minutes. Turn the pieces over and baste the other side.

Sprinkle with the remaining ¼ cup brown sugar.

Finish baking until the bacon is crispy.

Hot Bacon Chicken Dip

3-4 boneless, skinless chicken thighs or 2 chicken breasts

1 Tbsp olive oil

1¾ cup mayonnaise

8 oz cream cheese, softened

4 oz applewood smoked Gruyere, shredded fine

¼ cup dry white wine

½ cup green onions, thinly sliced green tops only

¼ tsp cayenne pepper or two shakes of hot sauce

1 tsp garlic powder

8 buttery crackers, crumbled

6 slices of cooked bacon, chopped fine or ¼ cup bacon bits for recipe pieces

1 tsp parsley flakes

Chop chicken into small pieces. Heat olive oil in small skillet. Cook chicken until tender.

Shred chicken and set aside.

In a medium bowl, combine cream cheese, Gruyere, mayo, wine, green onions and seasoning until smooth.

Add the shredded chicken and mix well.

Place in a deep dish pie pan. Add the crumbled crackers and bacon on top. Bake at 350 degrees for 15-20 minutes until the center begins to bubble.

Remove from oven and sprinkle with parsley flakes.

TIP: Serve with your favorite crackers or try corn chips for a change. Pre-cooked chicken can be bought and shredded to skip the first step. It takes 10-12 oz shredded chicken for the recipe.

Hot Gruyere
Chicken Dip

Kentucky Crunch

2 bags puffed corn, 10-14 oz total

1 cup butter

½ cup light corn syrup

2 cups dark brown sugar

2 Tbsp bourbon

1 tsp vanilla

¼ tsp salt

½ tsp baking soda

1 cup chopped pecans

Dark chocolate, enough to melt and drizzle

TIP: Put the puffed corn in a very large mixing bowl. You will need room to stir the coated corn quickly.

Prepare two baking sheets by lightly coating with butter cooking spray.

Combine butter, corn syrup, brown sugar, bourbon, vanilla and salt in a medium saucepan.

Boil on medium heat approximately 3 minutes, stirring constantly.

Pull the saucepan from the stove and add the baking soda which will make the mixture foam. Add the chopped pecans and stir well to evenly distribute.

Pour the mixture over the popcorn and stir quickly until the puffed corn has been evenly distributed with the mixture.

Divide the coated puffed corn between two baking sheets and spread into an even layer on each. Do not use parchment paper.

Bake at 250 degrees for about 45 minutes.

Stir often because the caramel will collect on the bottom and make hard pieces.

Let it cool on the baking sheets. Drizzle with dark chocolate. When the chocolate is set, break apart into pieces and enjoy.

Moonshine Chicken Bites

4 chicken breasts, cut into bite-sized pieces

50 ml or 1.5 oz white lightning moonshine

1 tsp salt

1 tsp black pepper

1 tsp garlic powder

**2 sleeves or about 50 buttery crackers
(Do not use saltines)**

1 stick butter, melted

½ cup grated parmesan cheese

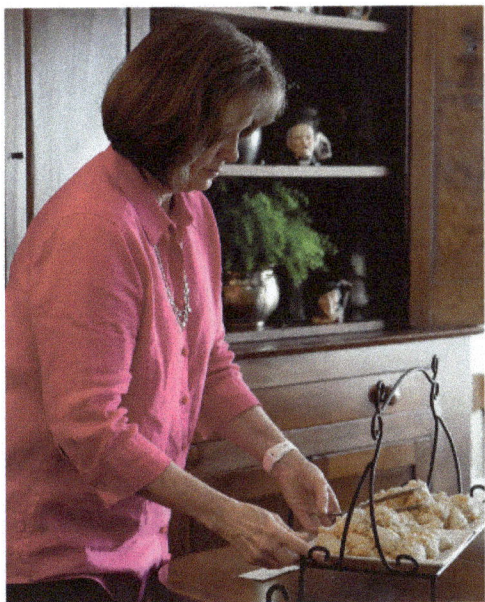

Cut chicken breast into bite-sized pieces.

Cover chicken pieces with moonshine, and just ½ tsp salt, ½ tsp pepper and ½ tsp garlic powder.

TIP: Covered pieces can be placed in a container in the refrigerator for two hours or overnight.

In a sealed bag, crush the crackers. Add parmesan cheese, and the remaining ½ tsp salt, ½ tsp pepper and ½ tsp garlic powder. Mix well.

Melt the butter in a small bowl.

Drain the marinade from the chicken. Dip each piece of chicken in the butter first, then roll in the crushed crackers.

Place pieces in a foil-lined baking pan. Repeat until all pieces have been covered.

Pour the remaining cracker crumbs into the bowl with the leftover butter and mix well. Crumble the mixture over the chicken pieces on the pan.

Bake at 350 degrees for 20-25 minutes or until the chicken is tender. If it begins to brown too quickly just cover with foil.

Peach Bourbon Slush

4 ½ cups water

1 ½ cups peach nectar

2 cups peach bourbon

¾ cup sugar

2 individual peach tea drink pouches

12 oz frozen pineapple juice (do not reconstitute)

Your favorite ginger ale or lemon-lime soda, or perk it up with prosecco, chilled

Raspberries, pineapples and peaches for garnish

Mix the peach tea drink pouches and sugar with 1½ cups water to dissolve.

Then combine with another 3 cups water, peach nectar, peach bourbon and frozen pineapple juice.

Pour into a large container with a lid and freeze overnight. The mixture will be a hard slush when you take it out of the freezer.

Stir to make sure all ingredients are thoroughly mixed as some separation will occur during freezing.

Place a raspberry in the bottom of a champagne flute, add two small scoops of frozen slush and finish with your favorite chilled fizzy drink.

I had my first Ale-8-One when I moved to Mt. Sterling, Kentucky. But my brother was already very familiar with Ale-8's and always picked up a truckload each time he visited the area. I should have listened to him sooner! I prefer this refreshing regional favorite to pour over the slush. Perfect for watching the sunset from your patio.

—Dayna

Sausage and Mushroom Swirls

2 cups chopped portabella mushrooms

1 cup sweet onion, finely chopped

2 Tbsp garlic olive oil, or regular olive oil

½ lb ground sausage, use your preference of mild, medium or hot

¼ cup red wine

1 tsp ground rosemary

2 tsp garlic powder

½ tsp salt

½ tsp black pepper

8 oz tube crescent dough sheet, or package of crescent rolls pressed together to make a rectangular sheet

TIP: Keep the crescent dough sheet in the refrigerator until ready to use. Do not roll out crescent rolls. Let the pastry stay thick or the sausage swirls will fall apart after they are cooked. Puff pastry can be substituted if the crescent roll sheets are not available in your local store.

Cook the sausage in a skillet over medium heat and break into small pieces while cooking.

When fully cooked, drain well in a paper towel lined bowl. Using more paper towels, place several on top of the sausage and press as much grease as possible out of the meat. Set the cooked sausage aside until the other ingredients are ready.

In a medium skillet, sauté onions and mushrooms in the olive oil until they soften. Add red wine and sauté another minute. Add rosemary, garlic, salt and pepper and sauté another minute.

Using a food processor or a blender, put the sausage and the skillet mixture together and pulse until it becomes a chunky paste.

Open crescent dough sheet on a sheet of wax paper to keep it from sticking. Spread with the sausage mixture to within ½ inch of the edges. Roll up from the long side until you have a tube of dough with the sausage mixture inside. Wrap with wax paper and put it in the freezer for an hour or more.

When you are ready to cook, take the roll out of the freezer, let them thaw about 10 minutes and then remove the wax paper. Slice into about 1/3 inch thick pieces and lay slices flat on a greased cookie sheet or on parchment paper on a cookie sheet.

Bake at 350 degrees until the crescent dough is light brown. Let the swirls cool on the cookie sheets for about 5 minutes before transferring them to a plate.

Savory Cheese Ball

5 oz jar sharp cheddar cheese spread

10 oz crumbled blue cheese

12 oz cream cheese

1 Tbsp Worchestershire sauce

1 tsp smoked hot sauce

2 Tbsp bourbon

1 tsp salt

1 tsp garlic powder

¾ tsp dried parsley

Whole or ground pecans as you prefer

Mix all ingredients with a hand mixer and form into the shape desired.

Roll in ground pecans or cover with whole nuts.

TIP: Pick some greenery to add the final touch. Wash and dry the pine well and cover it with plastic wrap before inserting into the cheese.

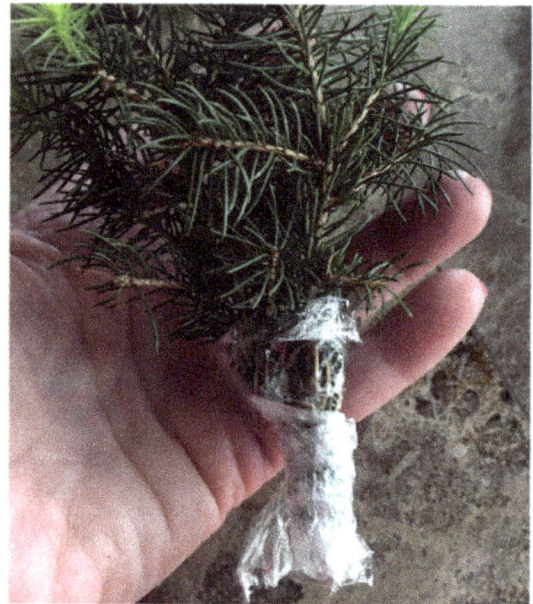

This cheese ball can be easily formed into a traditional cheese ball that can be rolled in ground pecans for a tasty coating. Feel free to get creative and try other shapes, like this festive pecan covered "pine cone", perfect to wow your friends at holiday gatherings. I especially love it because it freezes well and can be made up to two weeks before I use it if I am planning ahead for a family gathering or large event.

Smoky Bacon Pimento Cheese

3 oz smoked Gruyere, shredded

5 oz sharp cheddar, shredded

2 oz Old English or other processed cheese for creaminess

1 Tbsp bourbon

4 Tbsp bacon bits

2 oz diced pimentos, drained

¼ cup minced onion

1 cup mayonnaise

2 tsp sugar or 2 packets of Stevia

Shred the Gruyere and cheddar cheese into mixing bowl.

Add remaining ingredients to the bowl. Using a hand mixer, blend ingredients together until fully incorporated and creamy.

Place in an airtight container.

TIP: This recipe can be used as a dip, in sandwiches, as filling for celery or as a unique filling for deviled eggs as an appetizer. The flavors blend so much better if it is made the day before.

Sparkling Punch

Ice, small cubes or bagged, enough to fill a punch bowl halfway

2-liter bottle ginger ale

2 750 ml bottles champagne or prosecco

3 containers frozen white grape juice. (Do not add water. Use in concentrated form.)

Use a 3 gallon punch bowl for this recipe. If you use a smaller bowl, just scale down the recipe to your bowl size.

TIP: Make this punch about 15-20 minutes before guests arrive.

Using small cubes or bagged ice, fill the punch bowl half way up the side.

Pour ginger ale and champagne or prosecco over the ice.

Add in 3 containers of frozen white grape juice in concentrated form (do not add water).

Stir well and serve.

No sherbet in this one! I was never fond of punch recipes using sherbet. There was always an abundance of sherbet foam which left guests more thirsty than before. Living in Fleming County, Kentucky I drank this punch at almost every event. At most wedding receptions there was a "teetotaler" bowl made with all ginger ale and one made with sparkling wine. I can tell you the one with sparkling wine always disappeared first.

—Dayna

Main Courses & Side Dishes

The rock patio at the back of the beautiful brick home built in 1964 by Jane Anne and Emery Clark in Flemingsburg, Ky., is the perfect way to start your morning. The gorgeous gardens surround you, giving the feeling you are in the country with a sense of serene calm while you sip your tea or coffee and nibble on blueberry peach scones. Rock walls, stone pillars, and wrought iron railings and gates – shown on the back cover – provide lasting beauty that makes this house a haven of hospitality.

Bacon Maple Bourbon Dressing

1 Tbsp chopped green onion

3 Tbsp bourbon

2 Tbsp maple bacon balsamic vinegar

1 tsp Dijon mustard

2½ Tbsp dark maple syrup

1¼ tsp sugar

⅓ tsp salt

½ tsp ground pepper

¼ cup bacon, chopped fine

⅔ cup extra virgin olive oil

Place all ingredients into a food processor or blender and pulse for 30 seconds. A whisk can be used in a pinch.

TIP: I keep this in the refrigerator if there is any left. I just warm it in the microwave for 30 seconds before dressing a salad the next day.

Andouille and Chicken Gumbo

2 pounds andouille sausage, sliced diagonally in one inch pieces

6 boneless, skinless chicken thighs cut into bite-sized pieces

3 strips bacon cut in ½ inch strips

4 cups bone broth, chicken

2 large sweet onions, about 3 cups diced

2 large stalk celery, about 2 cup diced

2 green peppers, diced
(Remove seeds, stems and membranes)

2 Tbsp minced garlic

1 tsp salt

1½ tsp black pepper

1 Tbsp smoked hot sauce

½ cup all-purpose flour

½ cup canola oil

TIP: Timing is everything with this recipe. Everything needs to be sliced, diced, measured and ready.

Cook the bacon strips until the bacon is crispy. Remove the bacon and cook the sausage until the edges brown slightly. Remove the sausage and cook the chicken the same way. Drain sausage, chicken and bacon on paper towels to the side.

In a large pot put the bone broth, all vegetables and spices on to simmer while you are making the roux (below). Once the pot begins to simmer add the meat.

Gumbo starts with a roux, or thickening for the gumbo. Start with equal parts flour and canola oil over medium heat, stirring continually until it is a light to medium brown color. If it burns, just start over. Keep a flat spatula moving over the bottom at all times.

When the roux is ready slowly pour it into the simmering pot with all other ingredients. Stir often. If grease comes to the top, remove it with a spoon. Cook down until the consistency is a thick stew.

If a spicier version is desired more hot sauce can be added. Season with extra salt, pepper or garlic to taste.

Serve it with a lump of white rice on top.

BBQ Shrimp Salad

1 lb shrimp, deveined

Your favorite salad vegetables

Marinade

8 oz of your favorite smoky BBQ sauce

⅛ cup bourbon

⅛ cup dark brown sugar

2 tsp minced garlic

½ tsp salt

½ tsp pepper

1 Tbsp liquid smoke - hickory

½ Tbsp smoked paprika

Celery Seed Dressing

¼ cup sugar

1 tsp dry mustard

1 tsp salt

1 tsp garlic powder

2 Tbsp finely sliced green onion tops

⅓ white wine vinegar

1 Tbsp celery seed

1 cup olive or avocado oil

Prepare marinade by combining all ingredients. Place all but ¼ cup of the marinade in a container and add the shrimp. Make sure all pieces are fully coated. Marinade for 30-60 minutes.

Grill the shrimp over a hot grate for about 2-3 minutes each side depending on the size.

TIP: I like to use skewers to evenly cook the shrimp. They can be served on top of the salad on the skewers or removed and arranged on top of the salad.

Remove the shrimp from the grill and lightly brush with the reserve marinade.

For the salad: Prepare the salad base with your favorite ingredients. I love avocado, shaved parmesan, and red onions. Get creative and add the salad vegetables you love. Prepared dressings that work well with this recipe include sweet Vidalia onion or green goddess dressing. I have included my mother's homemade celery seed dressing recipe that has been a family favorite for all types of salads.

For the dressing: Add all dressing ingredients to a glass jar and shake really well before dressing the salad. This will dress about 8 salads.

Beef Bourguignon

2 cups beef stock

3-3½ pounds chuck roast, cut into large cubes

1 tsp salt

1 tsp pepper

2 Tbsp minced garlic

8 slices bacon, sliced in ½ inch ribbons

1 large sweet onion, diced

1 lb sliced portabella mushrooms

¾ cup red wine

¼ cup sweet vermouth

4-5 sprigs fresh rosemary
(or 1½ Tbsp dried rosemary)

3 large carrots, cut into 2-inch pieces

1 lb petite white gourmet potatoes or fingerling potatoes

4 Tbsp cornstarch (if gravy is desired)

Set aside the carrots and potatoes for adding later. Also set aside cornstarch if you desire to make gravy.

Using a large slow cooker, add the ingredients in the order listed except for the carrots, potatoes and cornstarch. Cover and turn on low for 6 hours or until the meat is very tender.

With about an hour to go on the roast add the carrots and potatoes. Try to minimize the time the cooker is open. Spoon some of the juices over the vegetables and cook the remaining time or until the vegetables are tender.

When the meat is done remove the meat and vegetables.

TIP: If desired, use 2 cups of liquid from the cooker and 4 Tbsp cornstarch to make a gravy that can be used with the meat.

Beef Bourguignon Meat Pie

Makes 2 pies

2 cups beef stock

3 pounds chuck roast, cut into large cubes (Remove large portions of fat)

1 tsp salt

1 tsp pepper

3 Tbsp minced garlic

8 slices bacon, sliced in ½ inch ribbons

1 large sweet onion, diced

1 lb sliced portabella mushrooms

¾ cup red wine

¼ cup sweet vermouth

4-5 sprigs fresh rosemary or 1 ½ Tbsp dried rosemary

1 large potato, diced

1 large carrot, diced

4 Tbsp cornstarch

Use your favorite pie crust recipe or 2 prepared pie crusts

Tip: This amount makes 2 pies but one pie can be made and the remainder can be frozen to serve with mashed potatoes at another time - two meals with one preparation!

Set aside potato and carrot for adding later. Also set aside cornstarch for gravy.

Using a large slow cooker, add the ingredients in the order listed except for the carrots, potatoes and cornstarch. Cover and turn on low for 6 hours or until the meat is very tender.

When the meat is done remove the meat and chop it into fine pieces.

Using 3 cups of liquid from the slow cooker, transfer it to a medium pan. Dice 1 large potato and 1 large carrot and cook until almost tender in the liquid. Add the meat to the pan.

Add 4 Tbsp cornstarch to make a gravy that is used for the base of the filling.

Using your favorite pie crust recipe or prepared crust, place one crust in the bottom of a deep dish pie pan. Add the prepared meat and vegetable filling. It will be thick. Do not overfill. Add the top crust and make sure you pinch the edges together firmly. Repeat with a second pie pan (or freeze remaining filling).

Bake at 350 degrees until the crust is light brown and the meat is bubbling. Store leftovers in the refrigerator.

We love this for a traditional St. Patrick's Day dish when made with ground lamb. We love it both ways. If you have a favorite mashed potato recipe please use it, but I have found the famous brand prepared mashed potatoes works great on this dish. For company this dish is perfect in individual baking dishes - my favorite is cast iron.

Beef Cottage Pie

2 Tbsp garlic olive oil

1 small sweet onion, chopped fine

1 celery stalk, chopped fine

1 medium carrot, chopped fine

1½ lb ground chuck

1½ Tbsp minced garlic

⅔ cup cut corn, frozen or fresh

1 cup beef stock

¼ cup cornstarch

¾ cup red wine

⅛ cup Worcestershire sauce

1½ tsp dried thyme

6-8 cups mashed potatoes

2 Tbsp butter, melted

Add the garlic olive oil in a medium skillet. Add the onion, celery and carrots and sauté. Remove from the skillet when softened and add to a Dutch oven or large pan but do not turn on medium heat until the beef is added.

Brown the ground chuck in the skillet, breaking into very small pieces. Drain the beef well after it is cooked then add it to the vegetables in the Dutch oven. Stir in the garlic.

Whisk the cornstarch in the beef stock until there are no lumps. Add the corn, beef stock, wine, Worcestershire sauce, and thyme into the Dutch oven. Stir until the mixture begins to thicken.

Once it thickens, place the beef mixture in the bottom of the baking dish or individual dishes and top with mashed potatoes.

Using a fork, make swirls in the mash potatoes that will hold the melted butter. Drizzle the potatoes with melted butter. Bake at 375 degrees until the meat mixture bubbles around the edges and the potato peaks begin to brown.

Bourbon Brisket Chili

1¼ lbs smoked brisket, chopped into small pieces

2 22 oz cans flavored baked beans, preferably a smoked flavor

2 16 oz jars of your favorite picante sauce (you choose the heat level)

8 green onion tops, chopped fine

¼ cup bourbon

2 Tbsp liquid smoke, hickory flavor

8 oz hickory smoked barbeque sauce
(Use your favorite)

2.25 oz brand name chili seasoning packet with onions

Combine all ingredients in a large Dutch oven and cook on medium for about 30-40 minutes. Because all of the ingredients are pre-cooked it takes very little time to prepare.

Tip: I make this chili a day ahead because it tastes better, as all soups do, the second day. It allows the flavors to meld together. I buy smoked brisket from a local grill.

This recipe also won a chili cook off against 11 other chili recipes. My husband, Mike, did make it all by himself using this recipe (with only a bit of support from his sous-chef wife)!

Bruschetta Pasta

16 oz Tuscan flavored tomato bruschetta

1½ lb ground chuck or lean ground turkey

1 medium onion, diced

1 Tbsp olive oil

¼ cup red wine, preferably dry

Salt and pepper to taste

2 Tbsp Tuscan seasoning mix - or make your own (see recipe below)

Angel hair pasta - prepare the amount your family likes for each serving

⅓ cup shredded three cheese blends (Parmesan, Romano, Asiago)

For homemade Tuscan seasoning: Combine 2 tsp garlic powder (do not use garlic salt), 1 tsp rosemary, 1 tsp oregano, along with ½ tsp salt and ½ tsp black pepper.

Using the olive oil, sauté the diced onions until softened. Set aside.

Brown the ground chuck or turkey. Make sure it is chopped into small pieces.

In a pan on medium heat, simmer meat, onions, bruschetta, wine and seasoning for about 30 minutes. Stir often to avoid sticking.

Top the prepared pasta with the meat sauce and sprinkle with three cheese blend.

Burgoo – A Kentucky Tradition

Large beef shoulder roast

8 boneless chicken thighs

6-8 boneless country ribs

1 large container chicken broth

1 pkg frozen corn, fresh cut is preferable

1 pkg frozen baby peas

1 pkg frozen sliced okra

2 large sweet onions, diced

4 large carrots, diced

4 large potatoes, diced

3 14 oz cans petite diced tomatoes

3 stalks celery, diced

1 Tbsp minced garlic

15 oz bottle smokey BBQ sauce

3 Tbsp liquid smoke

½ cup red wine

Use a pressure cooker or a slow cooker to prepare the meat until it falls apart easily. Debone and shred the meat and put it in zippered bags for the next day.

Save all the broth from each type of meat. Put the broth in the refrigerator overnight and remove the visible fat on the top the next day.

The next day, add all of the shredded meat, defatted broth and the remaining ingredients to a very large stock pot.

Simmer on medium until the vegetables are tender and the meat is "hammered" - or is in strings in the stew. This may take 60-90 minutes once it starts simmering. Stir often as it thickens.

Burgoo freezes great. This recipe makes enough to feed about 12 people with 2-cup servings.

Traditional Burgoo was made from any meat that could be captured or salvaged. Meats like squirrel, groundhog, rabbit and 'possum were used as well as the meats used in this recipe. It was a community dish served at public gatherings, political rallies and when friends and family gathered.

This was my favorite treat at Fleming County Court Days each October. Men would gather about 4 a.m. on the Courthouse lawn to start the large iron cauldron over an open fire. They took turns stirring, sleeping and swapping stories until it was ready to serve. The smell of the burgoo, crackling fire and the tradition of eating this out of a paper cup with my friends is what I remember each time I make this dish.

Chicken, Mushrooms and Bacon

2 Tbsp butter

8 boneless chicken thighs, cut into 3 large pieces each

1 tsp salt

1 tsp pepper

1 Tbsp minced garlic

½ large sweet onion, chopped very fine

2 stalks celery, halved and then sliced very thin

8 slices thick bacon, cut in ¼ inch pieces

1 lb portabella mushrooms, sliced

1/8 cup sweet vermouth

1 cup dry red wine (pinot noir is my favorite)

1½ cups chicken stock

2 level Tbsp dried thyme or 3 sprigs of fresh thyme

TIP: Do not use a non-stick skillet. Use an iron skillet or Dutch oven for the best flavor.

Preheat oven to 325 degrees.

Melt butter in an iron skillet or Dutch oven.

Rub salt and pepper into the boneless thigh pieces. Brown in the skillet until each piece is browned on both sides, then remove from skillet and set aside.

Add bacon pieces to the skillet with onions and celery. Cook until the bacon is crispy, and the onions and celery are softened.

Add mushrooms, garlic and sweet vermouth to skillet and cook until the mushrooms turn dark.

Add wine to deglaze the pan. Let the sauce come to a boil for 1 minute stirring frequently. Add the chicken stock and bring the sauce to a boil again.

Grease a deep baking dish, add the sauce, then place the chicken pieces in the sauce. Cover with foil and bake at 325 degrees for about 40 minutes.

Uncover and remove ¼ cup of broth and add ¼ cup of cornstarch in a small bowl. Stir to blend.

Stir the thickening into the sauce around the chicken. Bake another 15-20 minutes.

Serve over rice or mashed potatoes.

Cinco de Mayo Tacos

1 lb pulled pork or chicken, shredded

8 taco shells, corn or flour

1 ½ cup Thai chili wing sauce with 2 Tbsp bourbon, divided in two equal parts

½ cup cilantro lime salad dressing

2 Roma tomatoes, chopped

3 ears corn or about 1 ½ cups of cut corn

4 cups shredded cabbage with carrots and purple cabbage

Fresh cilantro for garnish, chopped into large pieces.

Cook the pork or chicken in a slow cooker until tender. Remove from the liquid and shred the meat.

Mix the chili wing sauce with the bourbon. Pour ½ of the mixture over the shredded meat and mix well.

Place three ears of corn in the microwave with the husks and silks on. Microwave on high for 7 minutes. Take them out of the microwave and cut off the stem end then remove the husks and silks. Cut the corn off the cob and place in a small bowl.

Chop the shredded cabbage into fine pieces. Make sure you have plenty of purple cabbage and carrots with the green cabbage to give the dish color. Mix with ¼ cup cilantro lime salad dressing.

Assemble in layers: taco shell or soft taco, shredded pork or chicken, shredded cabbage with cilantro dressing, fresh tomatoes, corn with the final layers, a drizzle of chili wing sauce and then a drizzle of cilantro lime dressing.

Kids love to make their own tacos. If you separate the ingredients into small bowls it is easy to make for large crowds and each guest can make their own. Provide guacamole, chips and a margherita and you have a party for Cinco de Mayo!

Fresh Basil and Corn Salad

Serves 6

6 ears fresh corn

1 qt cherry tomatoes halved

6 oz crumbled feta cheese

1 ½ cups diced red onions

¼ cup white wine vinegar

¼ cup white wine

¼ cup olive oil, use basil infused if available

½ cup chopped fresh basil, chopped fine or in small ribbons

Microwave the corn with husks on for 7 minutes (3 ears at a time works best). Cut off the stem end and remove the husks and silks.

TIP: For added flavor if you are grilling other items, place the ears on the grill long enough to get a small bit of char.

Cut the corn off the cob into a medium size bowl and let it cool while you are preparing the other items.

Halve the cherry tomatoes. I like to slice the red onions and then quarter them for medium onion chunks in the salad.

Mix the dressing using the white wine vinegar, white wine, olive oil and chopped fresh basil.

Combine the corn, tomatoes, feta cheese and onions until mixed well. Pour the dressing over the top and mix well again.

This salad is best if it marinates for about 2 hours in the refrigerator, and can also be prepared the day before serving. Set it out of the refrigerator for about 45 minutes to warm to room temperature before serving.

Fresh Corn Frittata

2 Tbsp olive oil

3 medium ears of corn on the cob, shucks attached

½ cup thinly sliced green onions

¼ cup half-and-half

¼ cup dry white wine

8 large eggs, beaten well

Salt and pepper to taste

½ tsp smoked paprika

1 tsp dried parsley or 2 Tbsp fresh parsley, chopped fine

½ cup three cheese blend, shredded (parmesan, asiago, Romano)

Fresh parsley for garnish

Select three medium ears of corn with the shucks attached. Place all 3 ears of corn in the microwave for 7 minutes. When finished, remove from the microwave, cut off the stem end of the corn, then peel back the shucks and silks. Cut the corn off the cob and set aside in a bowl. Slice the onions and add them to the corn.

Use a 10-inch iron skillet or other oven-proof skillet. Coat the skillet with 1 Tbsp olive oil and use medium heat. Cook the corn and onions together for about 2-3 minutes, stirring often. Remove from the stove and place back in the bowl. Add salt, pepper, parsley, paprika to the corn and onions and stir until evenly coated.

Wipe out the skillet with a paper towel to ensure any pieces of corn or onion that remain will not cause your frittata to burn.

In another bowl, whisk together eggs and half-n-half until completely combined. Add the corn, onions and spices to the eggs. Whisk again to combine well.

Coat the oven-proof skillet with 1 Tbsp of olive oil. Once the skillet has warmed add the egg mixture to the skillet. Cook without stirring for about 1 to 1 ½ minutes. Before the eggs completely set use a spatula to gently lift the eggs from the middle of the skillet and turn them over. If not, you may have a frittata that is tough in the center. Reduce the heat to low and cover the skillet and let the frittata cook for another 3 minutes. When you remove the lid the eggs should be set but a bit shiny on top.

Sprinkle three cheese blend on top and broil for one minute until the cheese browns. Garnish with fresh parsley and sprinkle with a tiny bit of paprika for color.

Tip: Use other fresh vegetables that can be found in the farmer's market. I have used asparagus, sweet onions, peppers, and spinach in the frittata. Have fun and design your own!

Grilled Chicken Kabobs

4 boneless skinless chicken thighs, cut in 2-inch cubes

2 large green peppers cut in small chunks

1 large sweet Vidalia onion, halved and quartered

4 Tbsp basil olive oil

2 Tbsp white wine

1 heaping Tbsp basil paste or 1 Tbsp dried basil

Salt, pepper, and garlic powder

Wooden or metal skewers

TIP: If using wooden skewers, soak in water for 30 minutes before using.

Spray the grill with cooking spray before turning it on to heat.

Sprinkle salt, pepper and garlic powder over chicken cubes.

Place chicken chunks, cut peppers and onions in a bowl with olive oil, basil and white wine. Stir to coat all of the pieces. Let it sit in the marinade for 15 minutes while the grill is heating.

Assemble the skewers alternating chicken, green pepper and onion and repeating until skewer is filled. Discard the marinade.

Grill on medium heat turning to ensure all sides get a bit of char. Make sure the chicken is done before removing skewers from the grill.

Nothing better than a cookout on a summer evening and a summer salad made with fresh vegetables from the garden or farmer's market!

—Dayna

Chicken, Basil and Tomato Pizza

11 oz tube or package refrigerated thin pizza dough

1 large sweet onion, sliced

2 Tbsp garlic olive oil

1 tsp garlic powder

½ tsp dried thyme

2 Tbsp white wine

3 cups chopped fresh spinach

8 oz chopped cooked chicken breast

¼ cup chopped fresh basil or ¼ cup basil paste (no oil)

⅔ cup garlic and herb spreadable cheese

⅔ cup pizza sauce (any favorite)

Campari or cherry tomatoes, sliced (enough to top)

½ cup three cheese blend (asiago, parmesan and Romano)

Salt and pepper

Slice the large onions in ¼ in slices then halve again.

In a large skillet heat the olive oil. Add the onions when the oil is hot and sauté the onions to caramelize and bring out the sweetness. About halfway through the process add garlic powder and thyme. When the onions are soft and caramel colored, add the white wine and stir for one more minute. Remove from stove.

Mix the chopped chicken, basil, fresh spinach and spreadable cheese until thoroughly mixed.

Use cooking spray to grease large cookie sheet.

Place the thin crust dough on the cookie sheet and spread as thin as possible without tearing. Precook the crust at 375 degrees until the crust begins to turn brown around the edges and the center is light brown. Remove from the oven. Spread the pizza sauce evenly over the crust.

Place the caramelized onions in an even layer on the pizza sauce, top with chicken, spinach, basil and cheese mixture. Lightly salt and pepper the top of the pizza. Leave no more than ½ inch around the edges so the pizza crust doesn't burn. Space the sliced tomatoes on top. Sprinkle three cheese blend evenly on top and bake until the cheese bubbles.

Cut in strips or squares to serve as an appetizer. This pizza is better after sitting for about 15 minutes as it is easier to pick up.

Mediterranean Pizza

11 oz tube refrigerated thin pizza dough

3 large onions (2 Vidalia and 1 red), sliced

3 Tbsp garlic olive oil

1 Tbsp garlic powder

¾ tsp dried thyme

2 Tbsp white wine

1 ½ cup crumbled Mediterranean Herb feta

1 ¼ cups Kalamata olives, sliced

**½ cup three cheese blend
(asiago, parmesan and romano)**

Salt and pepper

Slice the three large onions in ¼ in slices then halve again.

In a large skillet heat the olive oil. Add the onions when the oil is hot and saute the onions to caramelize them and bring out the sweetness. About halfway through the process add garlic powder and thyme. When the onions are soft and caramel colored, add the white wine and stir for one more minute. Remove from the stove.

Chop approximately 25 Kalamata olives in two pieces if small, three pieces if larger.

Use cooking spray to grease large cookie sheet. Place the thin crust dough on the cookie sheet and spread as thin as possible without tearing.

Precook the crust at 375 degrees F until the crust begins to turn brown around the edges and the center is light brown. Remove from the oven.

Place the caramelized onions in a even layer on the pizza dough, top with feta and olives. Lightly salt and pepper the top of the pizza. Leave no more than ½ inch around the edges so the pizza crust doesn't burn.

Sprinkle three cheese blend evenly on top and bake until the cheese bubbles and the feta begins to soften.

Cut in strips or squares to serve as an appetizer. This pizza is better after sitting for about 15 minutes as it is easier to pick up.

More Than Minestrone Soup

1 cup dried navy beans, soak per package instructions -OR- 15 oz can navy beans**

2 Tbsp garlic olive oil

2 medium sweet onions, chopped fine

1 heaping Tbsp minced garlic

8 cups beef stock

3 cups water

1 cup red wine

4 medium stalks celery, chopped fine

1 cup broccoli chopped fine

1 cup corn kernels

1 cup sliced okra

3 carrots, chopped fine

2 large potatoes or 10 new potatoes, diced

15 oz can petite diced tomatoes

1 Tbsp dried parsley or 2 Tbsp fresh, chopped fine

1 tsp salt

½ tsp black pepper

1 tsp smoked paprika

1 Tbsp Italian blend spices

2 tsp garlic powder

1 cup wild or white rice

If using the dried beans, drain the water off the beans, rinse in cold water and set aside.

In a large soup pot, sauté the onions and garlic in olive oil until the onions soften. Add broth, water and wine. Add the soaked beans and simmer for one hour.

** If using canned beans there is no need to simmer, just add the beans, vegetables and spices at the same time. Simmer for about 30 minutes until the vegetables are tender.

Add the rice and simmer for another 15 minutes until the rice is tender.

Serve hot sprinkled with parmesan cheese or cold (drain the juice) on a bed of lettuce.

Tip: If you are in a hurry you can use a 15 oz can of navy beans. Just rinse the juice off before adding them to the broth. This cuts down the time considerably.

My husband and I travel often eating wonderful, but heavier foods. When we return home one of our favorite healthy but extremely tasty soup includes vegetables, beans and rice. It is a comfort food in the winter but this thick soup is also good served cold over a bed of greens for a summer salad for light, refreshing meal.

Parmesan Jalapeño Tilapia

Serves 2 - Double recipe to serve 4

3 oz angel hair pasta

2-3 Tbsp olive oil (use garlic infused olive oil if you have it)

2 tilapia filets, about 5-6 oz each

1 cup chopped spinach

1 Roma tomato, chopped fine

Salt and pepper

4 Tbsp cornmeal

4 Tbsp butter, melted

2 Tbsp minced garlic or 1 ½ Tbsp garlic powder

1 ¼ cups heavy cream

⅓ cup white wine

1 ½ cup grated parmesan cheese

¼ cup finely chopped jalapeños with their juice

2 Tbsp juice from jalapeños

¼ cup parsley, chopped

Brush melted butter on both sides of the tilapia filet. Salt and pepper filets on both sides. Shake the cornmeal on a plate and pat cornmeal onto both sides of the tilapia.

TIP: Prepare the pasta before you begin the sauce. Drain it well when it is done and put it in a large bowl.

Have the chopped Roma tomato ready to garnish the final dish. Set aside.

Pour olive oil into a large skillet. Use medium heat and cook the tilapia filets until they become flaky but still hold together. Do not overcook or they will be tough. Remove and drain on a plate.

Add cream and wine to skillet and simmer until the liquid begins to bubble. Make sure you use a low temperature so the cream doesn't curdle.

Add garlic, spinach and jalapeños and simmer another minute. Do not add garlic at the beginning or it could turn bitter.

Turn off the heat, add parmesan and about half of the parsley. Stir well then pour half of the sauce over the drained pasta in a large bowl. Mix well to cover all of the pasta with sauce.

Place the pasta and the cooked tilapia on a plate. Pour the rest of the sauce over the tilapia and garnish with the remaining parsley and chopped tomatoes.

Tip: I slice and separate the thin sides of the filets from the thick sides and cook them separately so both are tender and flaky and the thin sides do not become dry.

Pepper Jelly Coleslaw

Slaw

5 cups finely shredded cabbage with carrots

1 cup yellow bell pepper, thin slices

1 cup red bell pepper, thin slices

½ cup red onion, thin slices and quartered

⅓ cup finely chopped fresh basil

Dressing

¼ cup basil pepper jelly

2 Tbsp peach bourbon

3 Tbsp olive oil

1 ½ Tbsp fresh lime juice

1 tsp salt

⅓ tsp black pepper

⅓ tsp red pepper (cayenne)

Place chopped vegetables and basil in a large bowl and mix well.

For the dressing: Right before serving, blend ingredients well with a whisk then pour over the coleslaw vegetables and stir until the vegetables are evenly coated.

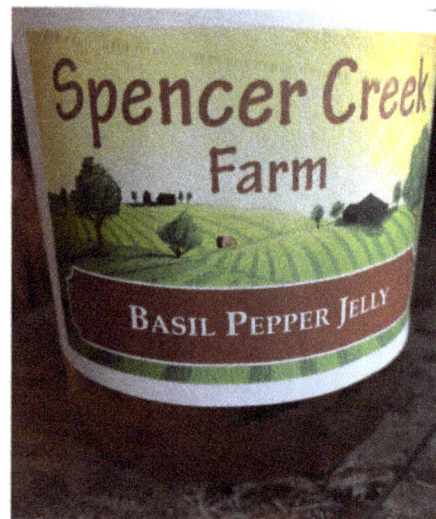

I adore the Basil Pepper Jelly I can purchase at my town's farmers' market. Martha and Darren Payne, of Spencer Creek Farm, have created all kinds of specialty jams and jellies I use in my recipes. Check your local markets to try spicy pepper jellies and experiment with tastes you like. The twist from other recipes is the peach bourbon which adds an unbelievably unique taste that pairs well with fish or as the topping for pulled pork or fish tacos.

Potato and Ham Quiche

1 ½ cups half-and-half

6 eggs

¾ tsp salt

½ tsp black pepper

4 Tbsp white wine

2 Tbsp chopped fresh basil leaves

4 russet potatoes, baked

1 cup cooked, diced ham

3 oz bacon bits

3 oz smoke Gruyere cheese, shredded fine

Bake 4 medium to large russet potatoes. Remove the skin after cooking and slice in thin slices.

Prepare a deep-dish pie pan with butter spray or melted butter.

In a mixing bowl, whisk eggs, half-and-half, basil, salt, pepper and wine until blended well.

In the pie pan, layer ½ of the sliced potatoes, diced ham, shredded cheese and bacon bits. Pour ½ of the egg mixture over the top. Repeat for a second layer.

Bake for about 30 minutes until the eggs are set. Test the center to ensure it is fully cooked.

Let sit for about 15 minutes for easier slicing. You can garnish with fresh basil or green onions.

Tip: Many recipes call for boiling the potatoes but I have found baked potatoes soak up the sauce and hold the quiche together. After baking the potatoes, the skin comes off very easily.

Shrimp with Creamy Wine Sauce

Serves 4-5

2-3 oz of your favorite pasta - linguini or bowtie work well with this recipe

2-3 Tbsp olive oil (use garlic infused olive oil if you have it)

30 small or 20 large shrimp, peeled and deveined

1 tsp smoked paprika

Salt and pepper to taste

2 Tbsp minced garlic or 1 ½ Tbsp of garlic powder

1 ½ cups heavy cream

⅓ cup white wine

1 ½ cup grated parmesan cheese

⅓ cup parsley

Put the shrimp in a bowl. Sprinkle with salt, pepper and paprika. Stir to coat well.

Prepare the pasta before you begin the sauce. Drain it well when it is done and put it in a large bowl.

Pour olive oil into a large skillet. Use medium heat and cook the shrimp until they are no longer translucent. The time will depend on the size of the shrimp. Do not overcook or they will become tough.

Add the cream and wine. Simmer until the liquid begins to thicken and coat the shrimp.

Add garlic and simmer another minute. Do not add garlic at the beginning or it could turn bitter.

Turn off the heat, add parmesan cheese and about half of the parsley. Stir well then pour the sauce and shrimp over the drained pasta in a large bowl. Mix well to cover all of the pasta with sauce.

Place the pasta and shrimp on a plate or bowl and garnish with remaining parsley.

Bob and Wendy Oppenheim, owners of Crystal City Olive Oil, introduced me to a variety of olive oils and balsamic vinegars. I use the infused olive oils in many of my recipes to subtly enhance the depth of flavor in the dish.

Summer Tomato Pie

Deep dish pie crust

3 large or 5 medium tomatoes, sliced ¾ inch thick

Garlic powder, salt and pepper to taste

½ cup finely chopped fresh basil

1 cup cheddar, fine shred

1 cup quesadilla cheese, fine shred

½ cup mayonnaise

¼ cup white wine

Slice the tomatoes about ¾ in thick. Place on paper towels to drain the juice. Sprinkle lightly with salt. Leave for about 30 minutes. If not, your pie will be too liquid.

Use your favorite deep-dish crust recipe or buy a prepared crust. Using a fork, prick the bottom and sides before cooking at 400 degrees. Remove the crust when it is light brown. About 10-12 minutes.

Turn the oven down to 325 degrees and begin to assemble the pie.

Start with a layer of tomato slices, sprinkle lightly with salt, pepper and garlic. Use ½ of the basil and ½ of the cheeses over the first layer of tomatoes. Mix the mayo and white wine together. Drizzle half over the first layer. Repeat for the second layer.

Bake in the oven until the cheese on top begins to bubble.

Cool slightly before slicing. This pie is good either hot or cold.

Tip: For a more attractive pie choose red, orange and yellow tomatoes to give it color. German tomatoes and Roma tomatoes have more flesh and less seed which makes for a better consistency in the pie.

Turkey Tetrazzini

8 oz linguini

1 medium onion, diced fine

6 Tbsp butter

¼ cup all-purpose flour

2½ cups half-n-half

1 can cream of mushroom soup (do not add liquid)

¼ cup white wine

½ tsp salt

½ tsp black pepper

⅓ cup grated parmesan cheese

3 cups chopped turkey or chicken

3 cups cubed sourdough bread

Butter a large casserole dish.

Cook linguini according to box instructions. Do not overcook. Drain well and set aside in a large bowl.

In a large pan, melt 3 Tbsp butter and cook onions until softened.

Add ¼ cup of flour and stir until thoroughly mixed.

Add the half-n-half, can of soup and wine until smooth. Remove the pan from the heat and add salt, pepper, parmesan cheese. Stir well.

In the large bowl thoroughly mix the linguini, chicken and sauce. Place it in the buttered casserole dish.

Melt 3 Tbsp butter in a medium bowl. Add the bread and toss to coat with butter. Top the tetrazzini with buttered bread cubes.

Bake at 350 degrees for about 30-40 minutes until the center is hot and bubbling and the croutons on top are brown.

When Thanksgiving is over, what to do with the turkey and 2 inches of wine in the bottom of the bottle? My family loves turkey tetrazzini and it takes care of both of those leftovers!

Kentucky Hospitality – Another Kentucky Treasure

The South is known for its wide porches, wicker swings, magnolia trees, colorful hydrangeas...and its hospitality!

Porches are for lazy days, cool drinks and good friends.

In the fall, the tradition is burgoo, horse racing and Court Days.

I was raised in Fleming County, Ky. As you entered town, you saw signs that said, "The Friendly Town That Hospitality Built". It has more than 200 buildings on the National Historic Register and is officially known as the "Covered Bridge Capital of Kentucky".

My husband, Mike, and I currently live in Mt. Sterling, Ky. We chose Mt. Sterling for several reasons, including the preservation of the historic homes and buildings along Main and Maysville Streets, as well as the revitalization of its lively downtown.

We fell in love with Mt. Sterling after we ate a chocolate croissant at Spoonful of Sugar and took a walk through the downtown area.

But the main reason we chose Mt. Sterling was because we were made to feel part of the community immediately.

Welcoming hospitality is seen in stores, on the streets, at our church, at events and in peoples' homes.

That is the treasure that awaits you when you choose Kentucky as your home!

Frances Roberts graciously allowed us to use her gardens for some of the outdoor photos in this book. The tranquil setting and gorgeous magnolias provided a grand setting for a garden party.

The Roberts residence, built in 1885, was known as the McNamara house. It had been vacant for approximately 20 years when Lon and Frances Roberts purchased the home in 2007. At that time, the house was so deteriorated that one could stand in the middle of the home, look up and see the sky, look down and see the earth. After extensive renovations to bring the home back to its grandeur, the Roberts moved in and enjoyed the convenience of city dwelling after living on a farm at the outskirts of town for over 30 years.

Desserts

Apple Shine Betty Pie

Use your favorite pie crust recipe or prepared pie crust

4 cups thin-sliced apples.
(I like Cortland, McIntosh or Winesap. They provide for a more flavorful pie.)

½ cup apple pie moonshine

1¾ cup sugar

¾ cup all-purpose flour plus 3 Tbsp

1 tsp salt

4 tsp cinnamon

½ tsp nutmeg

1½ stick butter

30 whole pecans. Do not use roasted pecans as they will burn while baking.

This is a combination of my favorite apple dishes. My mom, Carol, makes the best apple pie. It was a dessert we had often at our house. The first combination of ingredients is the mixture she uses in her traditional apple pie. It provides for a luscious sauce around the apples. The crumbly topping is used on family fruit crisp or cobbler recipes. And my brother and his friends love apple pie moonshine. This combination takes the traditional apple pie "over the moon".

—Dayna

Place sliced apples in medium bowl. Pour moonshine over apples and mix well. Let sit for about 30 minutes while you prepare the other two items for the pie.

In a small bowl soften ½ stick butter. Mix ¾ cup of the sugar, 3 Tbsp flour, ½ tsp of the salt, 2 tsp of the cinnamon, and ½ tsp nutmeg in the butter and then add to the bowl with the apples. Mix well until all the apples are coated.

Place coated apples in the prepared, uncooked pie crust. Spread apple slices out so they are evenly spaced in the crust.

For the topping: In a small bowl, soften 1 stick butter (½ cup). Stir in 1 cup of the white sugar, ½ tsp salt, ¾ cup flour and 2 tsp cinnamon. It should be crumbly. Spread the topping over the whole pie.

Place pecans side by side around edge of the crust.

Bake at 350 degrees until apples become soft, crust is light brown and topping becomes crusty. You many need to cover with foil if crust or pecans become too brown before the apples are ready.

Banana Blueberry Bread Pudding

½ cup (1 stick) butter, melted

1 cup sugar

¼ cup bourbon

5 large eggs, beaten

2 cups whipping cream

12 small croissants or 8 large croissants

1 cup chopped pecans (1/2 cup per layer)

1½ ripe bananas

1½ cups blueberries

TIP: This is best served with bourbon flavored maple syrup that can be found in many stores. You can make your own with ½ cup maple syrup and 2 Tbsp Bourbon if there is none in your local supermarket.

Preheat oven to 350 degrees. Butter a 13x9 inch baking dish or I prefer 2 loaf pans.

Cut croissants into 1-inch cubes and put ½ of croissant cubes as the first layer in the pans. Sprinkle ½ of the pecans and blueberries over the top of the croissant pieces. Slice ½ of a banana on top of the first layer.

Repeat for the second layer with all except the banana.

For the custard mixture: In a medium saucepan combine sugar and butter.

Add one mashed banana and combine well with sugar and butter. Add eggs and bourbon. Use a hand or stand mixer to combine well.

Add whipping cream and blend well.

Pour mixture over croissant pieces, fruit and nuts in the loaf pans and let it stand for about 15 minutes. Make sure all the croissant pieces are covered by the custard mixture. Press any pieces that are not covered down into the mixture.

Bake for 35 minutes covered loosely with foil. Remove foil and bake for another 15 minutes until the middle of the bread pudding is set, but soft and the top is golden brown.

Keep this bread pudding in the refrigerator until ready to eat.

This bread pudding is made in a loaf pan and sliced like thick slices of bread. I brown it in a skillet like French toast, top it with butter and bourbon maple syrup. A perfect gift for breakfast in bed.

—Dayna

Blackberry Crisp

This recipe makes 6 small ramekins, 4 large ramekins or one 8x8 crisp.

1 quart fresh or frozen blackberries

¼ cup sugar

¼ cup blackberry moonshine

½ tsp cinnamon

Topping

½ cup (1 stick) butter, softened not melted

¾ cup sugar

½ tsp salt

¾ cup flour

In a medium pan, heat blackberries, sugar, moonshine and cinnamon until the sugar is melted and blackberries soften.

Put equal amounts into each of the pans depending on the size you choose.

For the topping: Blend butter, sugar, salt and flour together well until it looks crumbly. Top each pan with an equal amount of topping.

Bake at 350 degrees until the blackberries are bubbling and the topping begins to brown. It will look like a finished pie crust.

Bourbon Biscuit Pudding

6 frozen buttermilk biscuits (do not use canned)

1 cup light corn syrup

½ cup sugar

⅓ cup butter

1 cup canned sweet cherries (drained) or ½ cup seedless raisins. Soak fruit in ¼ cup bourbon overnight.

¾ cup bourbon soaked chopped pecans (¾ cup chopped nuts and ½ cup bourbon soaked overnight)

Bake the biscuits according to the package instructions.

Crumble one biscuit in each serving glass.

Prepare the bourbon sauce in a pan on medium heat. Combine corn syrup, sugar and butter until the sugar is dissolved.

Cook for one minute after a rolling boil begins. Remove from the heat and add either the cherries or raisins and the bourbon-soaked pecans. Return to the heat for about 1 minute until it begins to boil again.

Remove from the heat and spoon over the biscuits. Generously spoon the sauce over the biscuit ensuring both fruit and nuts are in each spoonful. Serve hot.

I love my homemade buttermilk biscuit recipe but for this recipe I use frozen buttermilk biscuits because the sauce is the real star of this pudding. You can choose cherries or raisins as the fruit in the sauce. My taste-testers refused to choose their favorite so I have provided instructions for both. This is such a simple dessert that can be prepared in about 20 minutes and made the day before. Just put the biscuits in a sealed container and reheat the sauce before serving to your guests.

Bourbon Chocolate Chip Cookies

This recipe makes 48 large cookies, but can be halved easily

2 sticks butter, melted

1 block Crisco (1 cup) - Do not melt

1 cup white granulated sugar

1 ½ cup light brown sugar

2 large eggs

2 Tbsp bourbon vanilla

4 cups all-purpose flour

2 tsp baking soda

1 tsp salt

12 oz dark chocolate chips

Melt butter in a large bowl. Add Crisco and both sugars to the melted butter. Beat with an electric mixer.

When the sugar is creamed into the butter and Crisco, add two eggs and beat again just until mixed. Add the bourbon vanilla and mix one more time.

Add flour to the bowl, sprinkle baking soda and salt on top of the flour. Mix well until the batter is uniform.

Using a large spoon, add the chocolate chips to the batter and stir until the chips are distributed evenly.

Using a tablespoon drop the batter onto an ungreased cookie sheet.

TIP: Do not press them down to flatten. If you do, the centers will not remain soft. I make the cookies so they are as large as the palm of my hand.

Bake at 375 degrees until the edges just begin to brown. They will not look completely done when you take them out of the oven but will continue to cook for a couple more minutes on the cookie sheet.

Bourbon Cream Cheese Tarts

*Make approximately 48 small tarts
or 18 large tarts if cupcake tins are used*

Pastry

1 cup butter, softened but not melted

8 oz cream cheese

2 cups all-purpose flour

Filling

6 oz cream cheese, softened

1 ½ cups sugar

1 egg

1 tsp bourbon

1 tsp vanilla

Mix softened butter, cream cheese and flour together with a hand mixer.

Roll into small balls and put into small tart pans. Hollow out a crust with your fingers.

TIP: The mixture can be chilled if too soft.

For the filling: Soften cream cheese in the microwave for 30 seconds.

Cream all filling ingredients together. Fill the tart shells ¾ full.

Bake at 350 degrees for 20 minutes or until tops are light brown. The centers will puff up while baking but will collapse when cool to allow for the jam.

Let tarts cool completely and fill with one of the following options - or mix them up.

Carrot cake jam: Mix ¼ cup jam with 2 tsp bourbon. Place ½ tsp of mix on top of the tart and sprinkle with chopped walnuts.

Cherry preserves: Mix ¼ cup preserves with 2 tsp bourbon. Spread a small dab of sour cream on top of the tart and drop ½ tsp of cherry preserves mixture on top of the sour cream.

Nutella: Spread a thin layer on top of the tart and top with strawberry jam (mix ¼ cup jam with 1 tsp Bourbon).

Yummy cherry preserves are the traditional fruit used in these tarts. However, in the taste test group, the carrot cake jam and walnuts won hands down.

Bourbon Cream Chocolate Tort

Crust

½ cup butter, melted

1 cup all-purpose flour

¾ cup chopped pecans

Second Layer

8 oz cream cheese

2 cups powdered sugar

16 oz whipped topping

Top Layer

2 small packages of dark chocolate instant pudding

2 cups whole milk

½ cup bourbon cream

1 Tbsp bourbon vanilla

For the crust: Mix butter, flour and pecans together.

Press in the bottom of a medium baking dish or deep brownie pan.

Bake at 350 degrees for 15 minutes. Do not burn. Remove from the oven and cool completely before putting the second layer on top.

For the second layer: Combine cream cheese, sugar and whipped topping. Mix until smooth with no cream cheese lumps.

Spread evenly over the crust.

Chill for about 15-30 minutes in the freezer while you are preparing the top layer.

For the top layer: Beat pudding mix, milk, bourbon cream and bourbon vanilla until the pudding thickens.

Pour over the top layer, sprinkle with chopped pecans and chill for 4 hours or overnight before serving.

What to do with the leftover crust? My favorite part of the pie was the leftover homemade crust my grandmother would roll into a long strip, cover it with soft butter, then sprinkle the butter with cinnamon and sugar. She would roll it up longways and bake it along with the pie in the oven. I would frequently burn my tongue because I couldn't wait for it to cool!

Bourbon Cream Pie

**Your favorite deep dish pie crust recipe
or prepared deep dish crust.**

*TIP: Use your favorite deep dish pie crust recipe
or prepared crust. This pie will bubble over in a
regular crust. Prepared crusts that are not deep
dish will not be tall enough for this pie. If you use
those kinds of crust, roll out two together to make
sure the crust hangs over the deep dish pie pan.
Use a fork to pierce the sides and bottom of the
crust before baking.*

¾ cup sugar

1 tsp cinnamon

2 cups whipping cream

**½ cup bourbon cream and 3 Tbsp bourbon
cream**

¼ cup light brown sugar

¼ cup cornstarch

½ cup butter, cut into small chunks

½ cup walnuts, chopped

*TIP: Have all ingredients at hand and all steps
ready to go because this recipe moves fast
once it starts. Read the whole recipe before
beginning.*

Bake pie crust at 375 degrees until almost
done. Remove from the oven. Turn the oven
down to 325 degrees.

Cut butter into small chunks and set aside.

In a large sauce pan, combine brown sugar
and corn starch. Do not heat yet.

In a separate sauce pan combine white
granulated sugar, cinnamon, whipping
cream and ½ cup bourbon cream and bring
to a slow boil.

Pour the hot cream and sugar mixture into
the large saucepan with the brown sugar
and corn starch. Use a whisk to keep it
creamy. Let it boil for one minute over
medium heat.

Add ½ cup butter chunks you have set
aside and slow boil for one more minute.

Remove from heat and add 3 Tbsp
bourbon cream. Whisk to incorporate.

Pour into the partially baked pie crust.
Place walnuts around the edge of the
crust. The pie is also tasty without the
walnuts but the walnuts provide a more
eye-pleasing presentation.

Bake at 325 degrees for 20 minutes. Filling
will bubble like it is boiling when ready to
remove from oven. Do not overbake.

This pie is best chilled then set out at room
temperature for 30 minutes before
serving. Store leftover pie in refrigerator.

Bourbon Eggnog Custard

Makes 6-8 ramekins

5 egg yolks

¾ cup sugar

1 ½ cups commercially prepared eggnog

½ cup bourbon cream

1 cup heavy whipping cream

¼ cup bourbon

1 tsp bourbon vanilla

Using a hand mixer or whisk, combine egg yolks and sugar.

Mix the remaining ingredients in a separate medium bowl. Slowly beat these ingredients into the eggs and sugar.

Once thoroughly mixed, beat on high for about 1 minute.

Prepare a roasting pan with sides deep enough to add 1 inch of boiling water around the ramekins.

Place the filled ramekins into the roasting pan making sure the water doesn't come up more than halfway on the ramekins.

Bake at 350 degrees for about 35-40 minutes until the centers are set but soft.

Carefully remove the ramekins from the water and cool for about 15 minutes.

Cover with plastic wrap and set in the refrigerator for about 3-4 hours to cool.

Serve within two days.

Bourbon Ribbon Cake

2 boxes white cake mix

2 cups water

6 eggs

1 cup unsweetened applesauce

5 cups jam or preserves, up to 5 flavors

5 Tbsp bourbon

Buttercream Icing from Sparkling White Cake recipe

Prepare 3 large round cake pans the same size. For a square cake you can use three 8x8 brownie pans.

Mix each box of cake mix separately rather than combining. Prepare cake mix according to instructions, but use ½ cup unsweetened applesauce instead of oil.

Each box of cake will make three layers. Divide batter evenly among the 3 pans.

Bake at 350 degrees until the middle springs back. Check cake often while baking. Since layers are thinner, do not follow time on box or cake will be tough.

After first 3 cakes have been removed from pans, repeat with batter for 3 more layers with the second box of cake mix.

Cool the cake layers on parchment paper before you assemble the cake.

Mix 1 cup of jam or preserves with 1 Tbsp bourbon until smooth. Repeat until you have 5 separate cups. Use 1 cup of the mixture between each layer alternating the colors to make a prettier pattern.

Spread the jam thin to ½ inch of edge. Place next cake on top and repeat until sixth layer is on top.

You will use buttercream icing. (See the recipe for buttercream icing with the Sparkling White Cake recipe).

Ice the sides, then the top. Decorate with jam in the center. Cherry jam works well.

Cover and place in the refrigerator and allow the cake to absorb the jam.

Slice thin with a sharp knife and enjoy!

My Aunt Edith's jam stack cake was a treat at our Sparks family Christmas dinner. Since there were frequently over 70 relatives at our meal you had to be fast to get a piece - and I always aimed to be fast! Her layers were a cross between a cake and a crust. Aunt Edith was always able achieve 10-12 layers and cooked her layers on lard can lids. Her cake inspired this bourbon ribbon cake. I visit the farmers' market for homemade jams, have added Bourbon and aspire to an extra layer each time I make it. I have made it successfully to 6. Go as high as you dare!

Bourbon Tiramisu Bread Pudding

½ cup (1 stick) butter, melted

½ cup sugar

1½ Tbsp dark chocolate cocoa powder

2 tsp instant espresso powder (I use two espresso packets)

⅓ cup sweetened condensed milk

⅓ cup bourbon cream

5 large eggs, beaten

2 cups whipping cream

¾ loaf Brioche bread (chocolate if you can find it)

½ cup dark chocolate chips

18 lady fingers

Bourbon tiramisu cream sauce

4 oz cream cheese

2 Tbsp butter, melted

1 cup confectioners sugar

¼ cup bourbon

1 tsp instant espresso powder

For the sauce: Use a mixer to cream sauce ingredients together. Set aside to drizzle over bread pudding. If the sauce is too stiff to drizzle, microwave for 10 seconds at a time.

Chop Brioche bread into 1 inch cubes and set aside. Don't let this bread get hard and dry.

Melt ½ stick of the butter in microwave in a large bowl. Toss the bread cubes in the melted butter. Place two-thirds of bread cubes in the bottom of a 9x9 inch pan and sprinkle with ¼ cup of the dark chocolate chips. Reserve the rest for the second layer.

In another bowl combine the cocoa powder, espresso, sweetened condensed milk, bourbon cream, whipping cream and eggs. Use a mixer to beat until smooth.

In a small pan on the stove melt the remaining ½ stick of butter and ½ cup sugar on low until the sugar has dissolved. Do not let it cool or it will harden. Add dissolved butter and sugar to the cocoa powder mixture slowly while using the mixer. Beat for 1 minute on high after all of ingredients have been added.

Taking strips of the lady fingers, dip them in the mixture and place them on top of the first layer. Top with the remaining bread cubes and another ¼ cup of chocolate chips. Pour the mixture over the bread and lady fingers and let it stand for about 15 minutes.

Make sure all bread pieces are covered by the custard mixture. Press down any pieces that are not covered.

Bake at 350 degrees for 35 minutes covered loosely with foil, remove foil and bake for another 15 minutes until the middle of the bread pudding is set, but soft and the top is golden brown. Make sure the center is done. It should feel soft but not liquid when it is fully finished.

Top with bourbon tiramisu cream sauce.

Bread Pudding

½ cup (1 stick) butter, melted

½ cup sugar

1 ½ Tbsp dark chocolate cocoa powder

⅓ cup sweetened condensed milk

⅓ cup bourbon cream

5 large eggs, beaten

2 cups whipping cream

½ loaf Brioche bread (chocolate if you can find it)

4 chocolate cake donuts

5 oz dark chocolate sea salt caramel squares or bars

1 cup chopped pecans (roasted adds extra flavor)

Bourbon Nut Caramel Sauce

14 oz can sweetened condensed milk

1 cup brown sugar

2 Tbsp butter

6 Tbsp bourbon-soaked chopped pecans

TIP: The day before you plan to make this recipe, soak 6 Tbsp chopped pecans in 6 Tbsp of bourbon overnight.

Bourbon Turtle Bread Pudding

Chop the Brioche bread and chocolate donuts into 1 inch cubes. Set these aside. Don't let these breads get hard and dry.

Place two-thirds of the bread and donut cubes in the bottom of a 9x9 inch pan.

Chop caramel squares into small pieces and dot the bread and donut mixture with ½ of the chocolate caramel pieces.

Sprinkle with ½ of the pecans. Reserve the rest of the chocolate and pecans for the top layer. Prepare the second layer repeating the process.

In another bowl combine the cocoa powder, sweetened condensed milk, bourbon cream, whipping cream and eggs with a mixer. Use a mixer to beat until smooth.

In a small pan on the stove melt ½ stick of butter and ½ cup of sugar on low until the sugar has dissolved. Do not let it cool or it will harden.

Add dissolved butter and sugar to the cocoa powder mixture slowly while using the mixer. Beat for 1 minute on high after all of ingredients have been added.

Pour the mixture over the bread, chocolate and pecans and let it stand for about 15 minutes.

Make sure all the bread pieces are covered by the custard mixture. Press any pieces that are not covered down into mixture.

Bake at 350 degrees for 35 minutes covered loosely with foil. Remove foil and bake for another 15 minutes until the middle of the bread pudding is set, but soft and the top is golden brown.

Make sure the center is done. It should feel soft but not liquid when fully finished.

When the bread pudding has cooled and is ready to serve, top with Bourbon Nut Caramel Sauce.

For Bourbon Nut Caramel Sauce: Combine milk and brown sugar in medium sauce pan and bring to a boil over medium-high heat stirring constantly.

Reduce heat and simmer for 4 minutes, stirring frequently. Remove from heat and add butter and Bourbon-soaked pecans.

Let cool for 2-3 minutes. Drizzle on the cake while the topping is still hot.

My husband, Mike, made this cheesecake for his mother for years as one of her favorites. My mother-in-law's recipe box was recently found and opened at the 2018 Seelig Christmas dinner. This recipe had been lost for 20 years. We then made it together and I can confirm it is the best cheesecake I have ever put in my mouth. It does take a bit of time to make this recipe, but I guarantee after the first bite you will know it was worth the effort. I usually make bourbon cherries and also provide fresh strawberries so my guests can choose their preferred topping.

Cheesecake

Crust

1¼ cups graham cracker crumbs

2 Tbsp white sugar

3 Tbsp butter, melted

Cheesecake Filling

1 lb creamed cottage cheese

1 lb cream cheese

1 pt sour cream

1½ cups sugar

Juice of ½ lemon

4 whole large eggs

1 tsp corn starch

½ cup (1 stick) butter, melted

Bourbon Cherries

⅓ cup sugar

½ tsp cinnamon

3 Tbsp cornstarch

½ tsp salt

½ cup bourbon

⅓ cup light corn syrup

15-20 cherries, fresh, canned or frozen
(No maraschino cherries)

For the Crust: Grease the bottom of a springform pan and preheat oven to 350 degrees.

Mix all three crust ingredients together until crumbly. Press the mixture into the bottom of the springform pan. Bake the crust for 10 minutes at 350 degrees.

For the Cheesecake Filling: Mix cottage cheese in a blender or food processor until smooth. It is important there are no lumps.

Add cream cheese, sour cream and mix until well blended in the food processor.

Add remaining ingredients in the food processor or with a mixer until smooth.

Pour cheesecake mixture on top of baked crust. Pour to within ¼ inch of the top. The cheesecake will not bake over the top.

Bake at 350 degrees for 1 hour. Turn off oven but leave cheesecake in oven for 2 more hours. Take out and cool completely.

Refrigerate overnight. Go around edge of cheesecake with a knife before taking off the springform sides of the pan.

For Bourbon Cherries: Place ingredients in large sauce pan and cook over medium heat until sauce thickens. Cool and store in refrigerator to serve with cheesecake.

Cherry Chocolate Bourbon Blondies

½ cup (1 stick) salted butter, melted

1 cup light brown sugar, packed

1 large egg

1 Tbsp bourbon vanilla

1 ¼ cup all-purpose flour

½ tsp baking soda

½ tsp salt

1 cup dark chocolate chips

½ cup canned dark sweet cherries, drained and chopped into fourths.
(Soak in 1 Tbsp bourbon)

In a medium bowl, melt the butter. Add the sugar and cream until smooth.

Add the egg and bourbon vanilla. Mix well.

Add flour, baking soda and salt. Mix until all are incorporated.

Add the chocolate chips and stir to distribute evenly.

Drain the cherries and add them as the final item.

Press mixture into a greased 8x8 inch or 9x9 inch prepared pan. An iron skillet is also great if you want triangles for a hot dessert and a pretty table presentation.

Bake at 325 degrees for about 20-30 minutes.

TIP: They will be slightly soft until they cool. The center should be soft to the touch but not wet.

Cool completely and cut into squares.

Cottage Cobbler

½ cup (1 stick) butter

Fruit Mix

4 cups peaches

1 pt blackberries

¾ cup sugar

2 Tbsp all-purpose flour

1.5 oz peach bourbon

Crust

1 cup flour

½ cup sugar

1 ½ tsp baking powder

½ cup milk

Melt ½ cup butter in an 8x8 or 9x9 baking dish in the oven.

For Fruit Mix: In a medium pan combine fruit mix until it starts to thicken. Use medium heat so it doesn't stick.

Remove from stove and add peach bourbon. Stir well.

For Crust: In a small bowl mix stir together crust ingredients. Mixture will be sticky.

Use spoon to drop the crust mixture, dotting the butter in the bottom of the baking dish.

Pour the fruit mixture over the top, making sure it is evenly spread over the batter.

Bake at 350 degrees until the batter bubbles up above the fruit and browns on top. Bake approximately 35 minutes.

Dark Fruit Cake

Makes 3 loaf/bread pan cakes.

2 cups all-purpose flour

⅓ tsp cinnamon

⅓ tsp cloves

1 cup (2 sticks) butter, melted

8 oz brown sugar

5 large eggs

1 pound combined: candied cherries, pineapple, citron, lemon peel, orange peel (Choose a variety for a more attractive cake)

12 oz walnuts, chopped fine

6-7 oz each of the following dried fruits: raisins, chopped sugared dates, currants, golden raisins, apricots and/or dried cherries (Total of 2 pounds of dried fruits - all seedless!)

½ cup strawberry jam

½ cup molasses

1 cup bourbon

Mix the dried fruits with the bourbon in a large bowl. Cover and let fruit absorb liquid overnight.

Cream butter and sugar together with a mixer, add eggs and mix well. Add jam and molasses beating until smooth. Add flour, cinnamon and cloves and mix well again.

Add soaked fruit, candied fruit and nuts.

Using a large spoon, stir until all the ingredients are blended well and the fruit, nuts and candied fruit are equally distributed throughout batter.

Grease loaf pans, line with parchment paper and spoon in batter. This cake does not rise much so fill the pans to represent the size fruitcake slice you desire.

Fill an 8x12 cake pan halfway with water and set it on the rack below where you plan to place the loaf pans. Do not leave this step out or your fruit cakes will be drier.

Bake 2½ or 3 hours at 250 degrees. Be ready for your kitchen to smell wonderful!

Remove pans from oven and immediately take cakes out of pans and peel off paper.

After cakes cool, place them in plastic bags in the refrigerator. Refrigeration provides for best storage. If the cake dries out add more "moistening liquid" as the cake mellows.

Make sure when you add more liquid to use soaked gauze that has been wrung out, so the cake doesn't become soggy. You can use bourbon or sherry.

Cut cake very thin using a very sharp knife because of the amount of fruit and nuts.

Grant Alden, owner of CoffeeTree Books in Morehead, Kentucky shared his Great-Grandmother Heacox's Dark Fruitcake recipe with me and graciously allowed me to include it in my book. He remembers his grandmother baking this in a woodstove. I imagine it would have added even another dimension to the moist and flavorful recipe. I will admit I have never been a fan of fruitcake until I tasted this amazing recipe! My kitchen smelled glorious and the taste was like no other fruitcake I have sampled. She used sherry for her "moistening liquid" in the original recipe. In addition to the sherry, my taste testers also enjoyed caramel bourbon and straight bourbon to moisten the cake.

Eggnog Cake with Bourbon Custard Filling

White box cake mix, any two layer favorite

1 cup commercially prepared eggnog with bourbon, not rum (of course!)

½ cup unsweetened applesauce

4 egg whites

2 Tbsp bourbon vanilla

Blueberries, peaches or strawberries for garnish

TIP: This is an icebox cake that is prepared the day before it is eaten and stored in the refrigerator.

TIP: Use the Bourbon Eggnog Custard recipe in this book for the filling. Make this first and cool it in the refrigerator.

Coat three round pans with non-stick baking spray. Preheat oven to 350 degrees.

Disregard the instructions on the back of the box cake mix. Using the dry mix in the box, add the other ingredients and mix well with a hand mixer on medium speed for about 2 minutes.

Divide the batter between the three pans and bake until a knife comes out clean when inserted in the middle.

Cool the cakes completely. I like to freeze the layers overnight for a moister cake and easier handling.

The next day, assemble the cake by spreading the Bourbon Eggnog Custard between each layer. Because the custard is cold and the cake is frozen the cake will be easier to frost and handle.

Use the Buttercream Icing with the Sparkling White Cake recipe to ice the cake on the sides and top.

Add fresh fruit for garnish. Store leftover cake in the refrigerator because of the custard filling.

This cake freezes exceptionally well. Place slices between wax paper and freeze in an airtight container. Remove from the freezer 20-30 minutes before serving.

This is for my friends who asked how to make box cakes that would wow their guests. I love eggnog all year long and not just for sipping during winter gatherings with family and friends. Commercially prepared eggnog can be found in most stores beyond the traditional holiday season so there is no reason not to use it year-round.

Lemon Spirit Bars

Crust

1 cup all-purpose flour

½ cup butter, melted

¼ cup confectioners sugar

Filling

2 eggs

1 cup sugar

¼ tsp salt

½ tsp baking powder

2 Tbsp lemonade moonshine

9-12 raspberries

Preheat the oven to 350 degrees.

TIP: Do not grease the 8x8 inch brownie pan.

For the crust: Combine the crust ingredients then press the crust in the bottom of the brownie pan.

Cook until the edges of the crust turn light brown.

TIP: Prepare the filling while the crust is baking.

For the filling: Combine the filling ingredients except for the raspberries. Beat on high with a hand mixer for 3 minutes until very fluffy.

Pour filling mixture over the cooked crust. Place raspberries in the center of where each bar will be cut and cook until firm.

Remove from oven and cool before cutting. Dust with powdered sugar and cut into squares.

TIP: An alternate way to serve is to cook the bars and place the raspberries after they cool.

Welcome!
To Seelig B&B
Enjoy!

Malva Pudding

Cake

½ cup sugar

2 Tbsp butter, softened

1 egg and 2 egg whites

¼ cup apricot jam or preserves

½ cup heavy cream

1 cup all-purpose flour

1 tsp baking soda

⅛ tsp salt (pinch)

1 Tbsp white vinegar

Filling

½ cup apricot jam or preserves

2 Tbsp bourbon

Bourbon Peach Cream Cheese Glaze

2 Tbsp butter, softened

4 oz cream cheese, room temperature

1 cup confectioners sugar

¼ cup peach bourbon

For the cake: Cream sugar and butter. Add eggs and jam and beat well again.

Pour in heavy cream while mixing. Add vinegar and mix well. Add dry ingredients and mix with hand mixer for 2 minutes.

Place in a small baking dish or springform pan and bake at 350 degrees until a knife comes out clean in the center.

TIP: This cake will be medium brown on top when it is ready. You want this pudding cake to be tall so a small dish is important. You will be cutting this cake in two so you can spread the filling in between the layers.

Remove the cake from the pan, then let it cool for an additional 15 minutes.

Cut the cake into two layers and spread the apricot filling between the two layers and half of the Bourbon Peach Cream Cheese Glaze. Top with the remaining glaze. For extra flavor you can poke holes through the cake to let the glaze seep into the cake. I serve it with bourbon or peach ice cream for a delicious dessert.

I learned about this favorite South African dessert while on a river cruise down the Danube. My husband and I met two South African couples that raved about Malva pudding and encouraged me to "bourbonize" it. I loved these couples because they called me "Miss Kentucky" before they learned my name. The original apricot sponge pudding cake uses a vanilla cream sauce. I have added apricot bourbon filling and a bourbon peach cream cheese glaze. Sylvia, I hope you love it!

119

Peach Nectar Cake

Cake

1 box moist yellow cake mix

1 large box or 2 small boxes lemon gelatin (Do not use sugar free)

¾ cup peach nectar

¾ cup canola oil

2 Tbsp lemon extract

4 large eggs, separated

Glaze

5 Tbsp peach bourbon

1 ½ cups confectioners sugar

TIP: Do not use an electric mixer except on the egg whites.

Mix all cake ingredients together except for the egg whites with a large spoon.

Beat 4 egg whites with a hand mixer to stiff peaks.

Fold the egg whites into the other cake ingredients and put in a tube cake pan prepared with baking spray.

Bake at 275 degrees until a knife comes out clean.

TIP: DO NOT be tempted to turn this cake out of the pan until it has fully cooled or you will have to eat it with a spoon. It is just that moist!

For the Glaze: Combine glaze ingredients and spoon over the cooled cake.

Raspberry Cream Cheese Brownies

1 box brownie mix (use your favorite)

4 oz cream cheese

1 egg

½ cup sugar

1 cup raspberry pie filling

2 Tbsp bourbon

½ cup dark chocolate chips

½ cup chopped pecans

Butter or spray an 8x8 or 9x9 inch square pan.

Prepare brownie mix according to the instructions on the box. I recommend substituting ½ cup applesauce for the oil.

In a small bowl, whip the cream cheese, egg and sugar with a mixer. Dot the mixture over the top of the brownie mix in the pan.

Mix the raspberry pie filling and bourbon until smooth. Dot the pie filling on top the cream cheese mixture.

Using a knife, swirl the two together on top of the brownie mix.

Sprinkle dark chocolate chips and pecans over the top.

Bake at 350 degrees until the center of the brownies are set but still soft. Make sure the brownies cool fully before cutting.

This cake is for those who do not like – (gasp!) – chocolate cake. It makes a beautiful cake for a party, wedding reception or baby shower for a "reveal". The layers can be tinted with food coloring and decorated with spring edible flowers as a dessert for a brunch. This is also my go to cake for petit-fours as it handles well.

Sparkling White Cake

Cake

1 box white moist cake mix

½ cup unsweetened applesauce

¾ cup sour cream

¾ cup all-purpose flour

¾ cup sugar

½ cup water

½ cup sweet white wine or sparkling wine

4 large egg whites or ½ cup liquid egg whites

1 tsp almond extract

Raspberries and lavender or rosemary sprigs (Just enough for decorating cake top)

Buttercream Icing

1½ cups salted butter, softened but not melted

6 cups confectioners sugar

2 tsp bourbon vanilla

TIP: This cake is so easy to make and stays very white. I have also found it is the best cake for multiple layers as it is so easy to cut the rounds or squares in two layers.

This cake doesn't fall apart when you handle it and yet it is still extremely moist. I always freeze any cake a day before I serve it or ice it.

Prepare two 8" or 9" round pans with baking spray or shortening and flour.

Mix all of the cake ingredients at once. No need to use multiple bowls with this recipe.

Bake at 325 degrees until a toothpick comes out clean. Each cake will be split into two layers.

For the Buttercream Icing: Using a mixer, cream the butter, confectioners sugar and Bourbon vanilla until thick and creamy.

TIP: This icing recipe is so rich. Do not add extra liquid when beginning to mix. It will look crumbly at first but will form icing after a minute of mixing.

Ice the layers and the top and finish with the sides of the cake.

Decorate the top with raspberries and either rosemary sprigs or lavender sprigs. Dust with powdered sugar.

Spirited Fruit Tarts

18 frozen tart shells or your favorite crust recipe

4 cups diced peaches

1 cup peach jam

½ cup sugar

1 Tbsp lemon juice

4 Tbsp peach bourbon

3 Tbsp all-purpose flour

Tip: Make sure to use a fork to pierce the sides and bottom of the crusts before cooking. You can also use reusable ceramic pie crust marbles to hold the crust down. I like them because it helps the crust hold its shape.

Bake the tart shells for 10 minutes at 375 degrees. Remove from the oven and turn the oven down to 350 degrees.

In a medium pan on top of the stove combine diced fruit, sugar, lemon juice and bring to a boil. Boil for one minute stirring often. Turn down to a lower temperature then add the jam, peach bourbon and flour. Stir continuously until the mixture begins to thicken. Remove from the stove and let it cool for 5 minutes.

Spoon into the tart shells, filling almost to the top.

Bake until the fruit begins to bubble and the crust is a light brown.

Remove and let tarts cool for 15 minutes before serving.

We love all three versions. Here are two more you can try by substituting the fruit, jam and spirit.

Cherry tarts: cherries (canned cherries drained), cherry jam and peach bourbon.

Blackberry tarts (pictured at right): Fresh blackberries, blackberry jam and blackberry moonshine.

Strawberry Lemonade Cake

Cake

1 box white moist cake mix

½ cup pureed strawberries

¾ cup sour cream

1 cup sweetened coconut

¾ cup all-purpose flour

¾ cup sugar

3 individual packages of pink lemonade drink mix

½ cup water

½ cup lemonade moonshine

2 large eggs

Strawberries and sweetened coconut (Just enough to decorate top of cake)

Strawberry Buttercream Icing

1 ½ cups salted butter, softened (But not melted)

6 cups confectioners sugar

1 individual package pink lemonade drink mix

5 large strawberries, chopped fine (But not pureed)

Prepare three 8" or 9" round pans with baking spray or shortening and flour.

Mix all cake ingredients at once. No need to use multiple bowls with this recipe.

Bake at 325 degrees until a toothpick comes out clean.

Cool the layers completely before icing with the Strawberry Buttercream Icing.

For the Strawberry Buttercream Icing: Using a mixer cream the butter, confectioners sugar and pink lemonade drink mix until thick and creamy.

Stir in the chopped strawberries.

Ice the layers and the top and finish with the sides of the cake. Decorate the top with coconut and sliced strawberries

Tip: For additional moistness freeze the cake one day before you ice it.

Index

Conversion Charts

Liquid Equivalents	
1/4 tsp =	1 ml
1/2 tsp =	2 ml
1 tsp =	5 ml
1 Tbls =	15 ml
2 Tbls =	30 ml
1/4 cup =	60 ml
1/3 cup =	80 ml
1/2 cup =	120 ml
2/3 cup =	160 ml
3/4 cup =	180 ml
1 cup =	240 ml

Standard Cup Equivalents	Flour	Sugar	Butter	Milk
1/8 cup =	19 g	24 g	25 g	30 ml
1/4 cup =	38 g	48 g	50 g	60 ml
1/3 cup =	50 g	63 g	67 g	80 ml
1/2 cup =	75 g	95 g	100 g	120 ml
2/3 cup =	100 g	125 g	133 g	160 ml
3/4 cup =	113 g	143 g	150 g	180 ml
1 cup =	150 g	190 g	200 g	240 ml

Temperatures	
275 °F =	135 °C
300 °F =	150 °C
325 °F =	160 °C
350 °F =	180 °C
375 °F =	190 °C

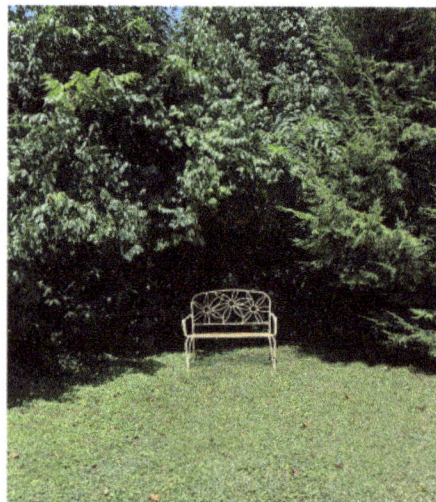

Small Town America

Kentucky cities and towns extend their hands of friendship and hospitality through all kinds of local events that bring people to our community homes.

Friends, neighbors, family and visitors gather to eat delicious food, listen to local music talent and have "street reunions" with family and friends.

My husband and I try to never miss Mt. Sterling's First Friday Market, Gateway Regional Art Center events, Small Town America Festival or Farm-to-Table Dinner.

I have been fortunate to participate as a guest chef in the Farm-to-Table event, preparing chocolate croissant bread pudding with bourbon cream sauce as well as spicy bacon pimento cheese and smoky bourbon sweet potatoes.

We love the Plein Air Painting event at Small Town America. Artists begin painting outside in our town in early morning and must finish their painting by mid-afternoon.

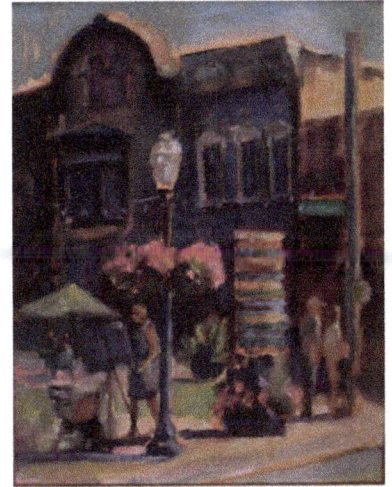

Cissy Hamilton Fine Art

It is interesting to watch the artists paint and create something so beautiful in such a short time. Painting is a talent I do not have!

These two paintings were done at Mt. Sterling's "Paint The Small Town" Plein Air event. They showcase the festive atmosphere when towns open their doors and say come in and play a while with us.

We purchased these two paintings — that we look at often — as a reminder of the open door that communities extend and the fun that can be had across this country...if we just get out in the open air and enjoy what our communities have to offer!

Frank Culberson Fine Art

Dayna Seelig is a retired professor of 27 years from Morehead State University. She was raised to appreciate traditional southern cuisine that included canning, preserving and cooking with her grandmothers. She was raised in Lexington and on a thoroughbred horse farm in Flemingsburg, KY.

Cooking and baking provide a relaxing outlet for her creative energies and she loves to watch her friends and family enjoy each other around a table of food.

Dayna lives in Mt. Sterling, Kentucky with her husband, Mike. Both sons, Rian Brown and Justin Brown, are wonderful cooks and have their own specialty items. And the tradition is being passed along to the next generation. The first question their two grandchildren, Hadlee and Quinn Brown, ask as soon as they come to her house is "what do we get to bake today?".

Dayna can be followed at www.kentuckyspiritedchef.com, on FaceBook: Kentucky Spirited Chef and on Twitter: @kyspiritedchef.

Jeffrey Liles is owner of Mound Marketing & Communications LLC. In his hometown of Mt. Sterling, Ky., he publishes the Mt. Sterling-Montgomery County Chamber of Commerce magazine and co-hosts Mound Magazine TV that airs monthly on Lexington, Kentucky's WTVQ ABC-Channel 36. Jeffrey was thrilled to be back working on Dayna's second cookbook. A dessert fan himself, there were many opportunities to try out the recipes that taste just as good as they look!

Dylan Lambert, owner of Dylan Lambert Photography in Hillsboro, Ky., rounded out the cookbook team. Dylan and Jeffrey had worked together on previous projects, and he had contributed photos to Dayna's first cookbook, too. Photo shoots in the Southern summer heat and humidity could be unpleasant, but when followed by a chance to actually eat the food, it makes for a good balance of work and pleasure.

www.ingramcontent.com/pod-product-compliance
Lightning Source LLC
Chambersburg PA
CBHW040247100426
42811CB00011B/1176